THOMAS GIRARD

EMERGING SCHOLAR

GRATITUDE OF AN AWARD RECIPIENT

This book was professionally typeset on Reedsy.
Find out more at reedsy.com

Contents

Contents

1

GRATITUDE 1: PRAISE

Thomas has served as an inspirational and productive force in my educational and professional career. As my design instructor at Emily Carr University, Thomas had and uncanny ability to challenge his students for the purpose of becoming proficient problem solvers, by encouraging outside the box thinking, and offering fresh perspective. Since completing the Interaction Design Program at ECUAD, Thomas continues to be a great mentor to myself and others. Thomas's commitment to his craft is astonishing.

– Cleveland Stordy

I feel extremely lucky to have had Thomas as an instructor at Emily Carr University. From the get-go he pushes his students to get outside their comfort zone and be the best they can be. You can feel he genuinely cares about his students and their journey to succeed, which was so refreshing and gratifying. I also appreciated his unique teaching methods, like the daily head dumps (which were a constant source of inspiration) and his hands-on approach to learning. He gave us the space to explore our creativity while always being available for feedback and direction when we needed it. Thomas is a natural-born mentor so if you get the chance to have him as an instructor, take it!!

  – Jennifer Phan

Thomas is an exceptional instructor and designer. As an instructor, Thomas is completely devoted to sharing his craft with his students. The way he teaches is engaging and genuine and he is extremely adept at getting students involved. His knowledge of UX design processes and patterns is expansive and he demonstrates this in the constructive feedback he provides. As a result, I have looked forward to every one of his classes and the ideas and methods I have learned from them have been fundamental to my design practice. Thomas also has an uncanny ability of identifying our strengths and weaknesses and tailoring our learning experience accordingly to maximize the potential of every student in the class. He is truly dedicated to ensuring that all his students succeed and he always makes himself available for extra help and mentorship, even outside of class hours. I am very grateful to have been a part of his mobile app design course. Thank you Thomas!

  – Brian Cheng

I had the pleasure of having Thomas as my teacher for Mobile Application Design. His teaching methods were inspiring and encouraging. UI research was never my forte, however after taking his class I learnt to enjoy the process. Thomas gave very useful feedback and really pushes his students out of their comfort zone and forces us to try new things. He's incredibly supportive and you can tell he really cares for each student.

Thank you so much Thomas for such an amazing and unique learning experience!
  – Caitlin Steward

I first encountered Thomas as my instructor for Mobile App Design in the Emily Carr Interaction Design Certificate Program. Thomas is a highly enthusiastic and perceptive instructor. He shares his unparalleled knowledge of design processes with the students in a way that builds our confidence while shaping our understanding. He has a talent for quickly identifying a student's strengths and helping them to advance their ideas based on those core skills. Thanks to his instruction and feedback, I feel ready to take on any challenge the field may throw at me. I strongly endorse Thomas for any creative and educational role.
  – Eva Prkachin

Thomas is a unique and creative instructor who truly wants to see his students succeed. His energy is infectious and his professionalism is top-notch. He took the time to learn about us individually as humans and professionals in advance in order to tailor the time in class to the needs of our group. He is a rare and wonderful teacher who creates an environment in which people feel supported, encouraged, and respected for their own areas of interest and expertise. He definitely does things in a very non-typical way which creates not only a great space to be in but really awesome results. Some of my best ideas and problem-solving processes have come out his class!
  – Kristine Bokitch

Thomas created an inspiring, safe space for me to be creative and take risks. The class dynamic was really great, Thomas has so much excitement and energy for his students, I felt like it made the whole class so much more excited to learn and to develop our ideas. In Thomas' class I was able to explore the process of a project from start to finish and gain more confidence that my crazy ideas would land, and when they did, how to organise them in a way other people could understand, too! Thomas' teaching style is really focused on trying things and iteration, which is really great because I often get stuck on ideas and wondering if they're good enough. In the classroom, Thomas got us to put our ideas out there so we could quickly get feedback from him and fellow students to see what worked and what could be improved upon. I learned so much about myself in his class and my ideas of my future became more focused. Thank you so much Thomas for being such an inspiring teacher!!

– Christina Loeffler

Thomas provides his students with one of the best learning environments I have had the pleasure to be a part of. He is genuinely interested in the success and participation of his students in both their educational and professional careers. As my instructor at Emily Carr University for the Mobile App design course, Thomas taught me how to plan a design project from start to finish, as well as proper techniques for creation of new ideas, Specifically overcoming obstacles, Paper Prototyping and User Testing. Thomas was always ready to chat about questions or concerns, or to give me feedback on projects. What I enjoyed the most from his methods of instruction are that he uses his students existing background to direct their work, which allowed us to created informed designs which turned out really well. Thomas was a pleasure to work with, and I look

4

forward to keeping in touch throughout my creative career.
  – Max McDonough

Thomas was my instructor during my interaction design studies at Emily Carr University. From day one, Thomas provided an encouraging learning environment that showed that he was invested in his students. As a student from a completely unrelated background to design, I felt that his instructional approach was inclusive and inspiring. I personally felt that his mentorship and carefully crafted feedback was very valuable to my growth as a designer.
  – Christina Lee

I had the pleasure of having Thomas as an instructor during my time in the Interaction Design program at Emily Carr University. Thomas is a wonderful, organized, attentive, and inspiring teacher. Right from the beginning, he was able to connect with and recognize everyone's strengths and weaknesses, and made sure to help everyone grow in their knowledge and abilities. He was constantly making sure to give each individual student attention and provided positive and helpful feedback, while maintaining a fun and safe classroom environment for everyone to excel. Thomas is a dedicated and passionate teacher, even arriving early and staying late to answer any questions, ensuring that we were supported throughout our project. His creativity and experience make him unlike any other teacher, I'm so grateful to have had the chance to learn from him!
  – Melanie Deschner

Thomas was my instructor for Mobile Application Design at Emily Carr University of Art & Design. He catered the course to align with each students abilities and it proved to be incredibly fruitful. In a single course taught by Thomas at Emily Carr, he inspired his students with drive, confidence and curiosity in user experience design. The development of each student reflects his ability as an instructor and mentor and it certainly did not go unnoticed. I appreciate all the feedback and advice Thomas provided and would be excited for the chance to collaborate with him in the future.

  – Sarah Tan

As a lifelong learner with several university degrees, including a PhD, I have been exposed to many instructors over several decades and it was with great pleasure that I lucked into having Thomas for two courses in design at Emily Carr University of Art and Design. Thomas has a special ability to not only energize a classroom with his idiosyncratic methods of teaching through head-dumps, "blue sky projects", hands-on exercises, and month-long app design projects, but more importantly through his ability to ignite a fire under each student individually. Thomas took time mentoring and guiding each of us; pushing and pulling us and our ideas. He was always at the ready for our questions and to help us through our road blocks, and was genuinely interested in our developing ideas and designs. I know I'm not alone in saying that Thomas has a real passion for teaching and learning and imparts that energy to his students. Sara Morison, psychologist, visual artist, and budding UX designer

  – Sara Morison

Thomas is absolutely, fully committed to the success of each student in his classes. He challenges his students to use their

6

existing background to inform their work and elevate the value of the group's time in studio, and helps students identify blocks that will limit them as designers. He encourages students to push themselves past the limits they once thought possible, supports them by reviewing portfolio work and resumes, and makes industry introductions where appropriate.

– Katrina Heschel

Thomas is an incredible leader, mentor and teacher, who is really invested in his students careers. I saw these qualities first hand, when he was our mentor in a 24 hour hackathon. In the time pressure our team had, Thomas stepped in and steered our team in the right direction. Providing us with strategic and design direction, when our team needed it the most. He fosters a truly collaborative environment in his classroom, and always brings about the newest design trends and practices to the forefront. I am incredibly grateful to have Thomas as a teacher and mentor, in my design career. He is a visionary and a thought leader, who I would highly recommend, for any role.

– Shua Baber

I had the pleasure of having Thomas as an instructor for the Mobile Application Design course at Emily Carr University. Thomas really cared about his students' success and his positive energy created an environment where students feel encouraged and supported. Throughout the course I really appreciated Thomas' ability recognize our strengths and his encouragement to utilize our strengths in the design process. Thomas provided a safe space for everyone in class to get outside of their comfort zone to explore and problem-solve. He took time to mentor each of us individually and provided reflective feedback which further

7

pushed us past limits we once thought existed. Thomas is an inspiring mentor and his instructional method was immensely helpful in fostering my creative confidence!

– Rei Ahn

Thomas provided very useful feedback for me for a major project I worked on. He is an excellent source for guidance if you need help on anything you work on with his high insight to interaction design. He will be a big plus to any industry he enters with his vast knowledge in designing experience for various audiences. He also has amazing ability to adapt to different environments, as well as catering to different individual needs.

– Kevin Park

It has been a pleasure to have Thomas as my instructor for the Mobile Application Design course at Emily Carr. He provides a welcoming and supportive environment where everyone can discuss and explore challenges and possibilities. His ways of incorporating new teaching strategies into lessons reflect his passion for design and education. My conversations with Thomas has made an impact on the way I think of creating a valuable user experience.

– Patrick Espiritu

Thomas has been an invaluable mentor to me, he has helped me grow both as a young designer and as a person. I first met Thomas while enrolled in the Emily Carr Interaction Design Essentials program where he taught Mobile Application Design. I am now studying in London at Ravensbourne University as a Product Designer. Thomas is committed to making sure I am constantly improving my work by consistently checking in with me, providing feedback and critique which I have found helpful and quite necessary. Thomas has been supportive, kind and has aided me without any ask for anything in return – I believe this is his most admirable trait; his desire to help all of his students with remarkable care and attention. I hope this speaks to what a great mentor and friend Thomas is, I am very glad to have met him and would recommend him wholeheartedly.

  – Hafeez Dawood

Thomas' mentorship is unparalleled to any other I've experienced. He has an incredible talent for creating emotional value which is such a huge part of the user journey. Furthermore, I was very impressed with his creative methods of moving through the ideation process. I count myself lucky to have learned so much from Thomas within such a short span of time.

  – Jared Zecchel

During my time at Emily Carr, I had the pleasure of having Thomas as one of my instructor's in Interaction Design. He truly cared about the success of his students and continuously provided us with different tools and techniques to carry out our work. He was always available for guidance and support. Thomas encouraged collaboration and innovation, allowing us to take our creativity to a new level. He is a true gem in the industry.

  – Alice Vax

Thomas was my instructor for several courses during my time at Emily Carr. He was an excellent mentor who was able to inspire me to push my creative thinking and abilities. His dedication to helping every student showed and he was always very willing

9

to give up his personal time to offer individual help to every student. Overall, I believe that Thomas is was an integral part to my learning and development throughout the entire program.

– Natalie Lim

Thomas was my instructor for Mobile App Design at Emily Carr University of Art & Design. It was very evident upon first meeting him that being a designer is more than just his job, but a way of life. He has a strong commitment to refining his own practice, and this dedication inspires his students to follow his lead. What I appreciate most about Thomas is how much time and space he gives students to take their ideas, and run with them. He provides direction when necessary, but it is usually open to interpretation, which allows students to develop their own unique design process. Skills I have learned from Thomas' class will serve me throughout my entire career, regardless of where it takes me. I would highly recommend him as an instructor, and a design professional.

– Hilary Romans

I was lucky to have Thomas as my instructor for Mobile App Design at Emily Carr University of Art & Design. From day one, Thomas showed such commitment to the success of each and every one of his students. Thomas' innovative and collaborative teaching style created a space where students felt inspired, challenged, encouraged and valued. He was genuinely interested in our developing ideas and designs and was always ready to chat and answer questions or give feedback. It is rare that you come across an instructor like Thomas. The best of the best.

– Sarah Bartley

Thomas is committed to helping all of his students achieve their individual goals through his design experience and industry connections. He has a lot to offer his students if they are willing to seek his assistance. As a recent graduate of the University of Waterloo with a bachelors degree in Knowledge Integration (a collaborative interdisciplinary program) with a varied background in work and design experience, Thomas has helped me narrow my focus and better understand potential career paths. He has gone out of his way to help me focus on future directions and helped align the work I am doing in class with career goals. Thomas's classes at Emily Carr leave a lot of room to explore and push boundaries. He is knowledgeable, articulate, and very open-minded when giving critique and feedback making his classroom a very safe space to design in freely. I look forward to designing and learning from Thomas in second term.

  – Clarice Chin

My first encounter with Thomas was at Emily Carr University during the Continuing Studies Interaction Design certificate. He taught Mobile App Design during my second semester. Thomas got personally invested in everyone's projects and genuinely wanted everyone to succeed. Thomas has an amazing view on design concepts, patterns and was very clear during all of his lectures and presentations. His class was very hands on and gave me the time to be challenged and experiment with different design concepts, but most of all, truly understand. In the duration of this course, I started developing one of portfolio pieces and it will turn into the perfect project, thanks to Thomas. I am thoroughly enjoying the time I have in Thomas' class.

  – Alison Stewart-Patterson

I met Thomas while enrolled in the Emily Carr Interaction Design Essentials program where he taught Mobile App Design. His authenticity and professionalism in teaching the class are far beyond the normal way of teaching. Thomas's methods are rich, yet easy to follow, allowing his students to engage and perform at their best. He was able to bring out my personality and creativity by giving me space to explore. He is always available for feedback and direction when I needed it. He is dedicated to helping all his students succeed, going above and beyond to mentor us both in and out of the classroom. Thomas is a natural mentor, and I am glad that I have met him.

   – Lilian Salloum

I was so lucky to have Thomas as my instructor for mobile app class at Emily Carr University. He is a great talented designer, artist, creative problem solver and an ethousiastic instuctor who is always try to share his knowledge with his students with out any deficiency. I found him as a teacher who always dedicated to help and courage his students to grow based on their skills and experiences to be successful. Thomas was not only my unique instructor also one of my good friends.

   – Mona Meysami

Thomas was my instructor for Mobile Application Design at Emily Carr University of Art & Design. I would like to say in confidence that Thomas is a great instructor and an inspiring figure – he truly knows how to naturally create a supportive and learning environment where students feel encouraged to share ideas, help each other, and grow together as a team. In addition, he is great at bringing out each student's strengths and abilities by catering his class to align with each student's experiences. He is also an excellent source for guidance – Thomas always answered my questions promptly and gave me a lot of resources and insights to push my projects forward. I can't thank him enough for all his support, input and encouragement!

– Heart Cho

I had Thomas as a professor for the Mobile App Design course during my time at Emily Carr. He showed expertise in the UX process through his personalized guidance playing to each individual student's skill set. He has aided me in making use of creativity and logic when designing, while keeping the end user in mind. It is obvious that Thomas genuinely cares about the success of his students by going above and beyond, whether that means staying late after class, or coming in on a Sunday to judge a student led competition. He continually proves there's a vast difference between a teacher and an educator.

– Nicole Alexandra Waldern

Thomas is a very committed and thoughtful mentor that I was lucky to have throughout my experience at Emily Carr University's interaction design program. His passion for design thinking manifests through his work and in his teaching style. Thomas is a proactive and approachable mentor who reaches out to all of his students in order to help them succeed. I highly recommend Thomas because he is an observant person who has helped me undergo tremendous growth in my own education in design.

– Emily Han

During my time in the interaction design programme at Emily

Carr, I had the pleasure of working with Thomas. He is a driven and organized instructor who develops stimulating relationships with his students. His unique teaching style allows students to explore multiple iterations of their concept, while working in a highly collaborative environment. Thomas uses his extensive experience to introduce many valuable insights into the user experience industry. During class sessions, I have seen Thomas give extra attention to each student, in order to develop their unique strengths. In addition, he is always available before and after class to provide support and guidance. Thomas' innovative and collaborative teaching style has provided great value to my creative experience.

– Ayoob Ullah

Thomas is an amazing instructor who has the unique ability to help students understand abstract ideas in a very simple way. He is extremely creative in his teaching style and is very dedicated to his craft. I had the privilege of being in his classes at Emily Carr University which elevated my skills as a designer. His talent in the industry is translated into the classroom where he pushes the boundaries of art and technology and motivates each student to be at their best. Thomas brings a fresh perspective to every session and goes above and beyond to help his students think in a different way. His depth of knowledge and dedication to design is thoughtful and rewarding. Thomas embodies what every instructor aspires to be, and inspires anyone interested in design to realize what is possible. His mentorship and guidance as an instructor is unmatched.

– Andrea Mah

I had the pleasure of taking several classes with Thomas during my time in Emily Carr University's interaction design program. Coming from an Ivy League liberal arts background, I was challenged by Thomas' teaching style to think and create in a way I had never before. Integrating conceptual development with a variety of hands-on techniques, Thomas provided an environment for students to stretch their skills base and build confidence in their creative process. Extending beyond design, his methods are relevant in any field where one needs to communicate and reach a targeted audience effectively. Above all, Thomas is a great mentor who generously supports students in their career development, both during and after the program.

– Misty Liang

I too was lucky enough to have Thomas as my mobile app design and UX teacher. He taught us current trends and methods of design thinking, prototyping, user testing, and each of their respective importances in modern design. He fostered a great learning environment and he regularly encouraged us as a group to get together and share our successes and frustrations with our post-schooling careers. Not only does he do a great job teaching, but he genuinely cares! 10/10

– Brian Corber

Thomas is a passionate and committed mentor that helps his students achieve their potentials and become who they want to be. My background is in Industrial design and I used to work as a UI and graphic designer before I move to Vancouver. I decided to study Interaction design at Emily Carr to develop my skills and to connect with designers in Vancouver. Thomas was one of my first teachers that helped me to trust my skills and knowledge and to value them as unique qualities. He encourages students

15

to experience, take risks and connect with other designer. He is very smart and recognizes his student's talents and encourages them to develop these qualities. Moreover, I found Thomas to be a really nice guy who is generous in sharing his knowledge with students and provides the opportunity for them to practice sharing their knowledge in return.

  – Maryam Azarnia

Thomas is a very thoughtful, genuine and observant individual. His feedback was crucial for me in my professional growth as a designer and how I would take steps beyond Emily Carr into the industry. Our conversations throughout my internship application process to FCV was incredibly helpful as he shared what it was like to be a budding designer and how to follow up with formality but keen interest while keeping in mind about the company's timeline. This made my application process a lot less stressful. I continue to keep in touch with Thomas and there is good reason why. He is a truly keen and passionate individual that believes in the power of Design and Design thinking and mentoring students beyond the classroom.

  – Shiaoshiao Chen

Thomas has a genuine passion for all things design – this enabled him to build an interesting and varied course structure. He excited our class by allowing us to design 'blue sky' ideas, but then grounded us in reality by presenting true-to-life development/client scenarios. He fostered an open culture of sharing with daily 'brain dumps' for students to either absorb or contribute design knowledge. I really felt he gave us the opportunity to shine while provided us useful techniques, tools and insights to bring into the real world. Lastly, his unique and sometimes quirky personality was refreshing among the monotonous lectures and homework of student life. Great experience overall!

  – Sam Flores

I was lucky enough to have Thomas as my user experience design teacher. He taught us the process of design thinking, real world prototyping, user testing, and their importance. No exaggeration, he's one of the best teachers I've had, and I regularly apply the methodologies he shared with us.

  – Craig Huff

Thomas is smart, perceptive, caring, and deeply committed to helping his students succeed, calling on them to challenge themselves when in school as well as to unreservedly pursue learning beyond it. His positive outlook and sincere belief in community are catching, and have led his students to establish meaningful connections with each other that spread far beyond each graduating class. His approach pushes students to further their thinking, take action on their career aspirations, and undergo remarkable growth as a result. He has a knack for drawing out students' unique strengths and bringing them into dialogue together so that each plays off the others to lift all. Thomas's emphasis on teaching design thinking, process, and methodology helped me build on my own existing educational and professional experiences in ways I couldn't previously have anticipated, and following my studies at Emily Carr, I was accepted into the MA Information Design program at the University of Reading's Department of Typography and Graphic Communication.

  – Andrea Wong

17

Thomas communicates a deep knowledge and instinct for the iterative design process. It was a pleasure to study under his tutelage for 6 months. Learning a vast range of design methods and processes that really helped me in strategizing and reaching my goals. Thomas is patient, thoughtful, and a enjoyable team leader that really strives for the betterment of the whole and each individual based on an assessment of skills and interests. He has the ability to help you understand a subject from multiple perspectives and use your own mind to produce amazing insights, helping you really construct original and practical approaches to solving really any problem. Thomas was a joy, and made himself available at all times for feedback, or help guide everyone.

– Kyle Saint-Amour Brennan

Great teachers become immortal _ they make undeniable impacts on their students, and Thomas is without doubt one of them. He is an incredible person and an amazing teacher, and it was a great privilege for me to be in his Interaction Design classes at Emily Carr. Thomas is a devoted instructor who truly cares about each and every student he comes into contact with. You can often find him in his classroom outside class hours, making himself available to those who need help. When teaching, he is not only extremely knowledgeable and experienced but also has the ability to bring the subject to life through interesting and meaningful activities. That is why the entire class immensely enjoys interacting with him. To me, he is an inspiration and instrumental in developing my skills as a designer.

– Mo Torabi

It's rare that you come across an instructor such as Thomas. He has tremendous initiative, a desire to continue to learn and a willingness to modify his teaching methods based on his class's needs and personalities. He consistently does this by observing and adapting a no "ego" approach about preferred teaching styles. I have had the enjoyment of experiencing this first hand at Emily Carr University participating in classes such as Design Fundamentals and Mobile App Design. Thomas displays the qualities that make a teacher successful. He is dependent, motivated and in tune with the needs of his students. I am very grateful and would like to thank Thomas for his invaluable support and mentorship on my successes as a Web Design Freelancer.

    – Jennifer Mills

Thomas was an exceptional instructor. He always took his teaching beyond the classroom. He would meet one-on-one with students, encourage them based on their individual skill, challenge them to grow, and help them pursue career opportunities even after our classes with him were complete. Thomas posesses the traits of a great professor of design: someone who is not only thoughtful and critical, but also caring and fun. He is exceptionally knowledgable about all aspects of design and industry trends. I would highly recommend him as a professor of design.

    – Katie Alcock

I was extremely lucky to have Thomas as my instructor for Design for Design Fundamentals and Mobile App Design during my Interactive Design Essentials program at Emily Carr. He was not only very knowledgeable but also very dedicated to helping all his students succeed, often going above and beyond to mentor

19

us both in and out of classroom. Not only did Thomas impart
to us his knowledge and experience in interaction design, he
challenged and encouraged us to apply what we have learnt
outside of the classroom setting at events such as hackathons. I
am very thankful for Thomas's ongoing support and mentorship
throughout and beyond the IDES program.

  – Mimi Xia

I came to the Interaction Design Essentials program at ECUAD
after completing an undergraduate Liberal Arts degree at Quest
University Canada, where I focused on technology politics and
cognition. I was lucky enough to work closely with faculty during
my undergraduate degree, and can confidently say Thomas is
one of the most excellent and committed educators I've ever
had the pleasure of working with. He has made himself available
beyond expectation in order to help me develop as a designer
by sharing resources, offering advice, creating connections,
providing meaningful critiques of my work, and challenging
my opinions and perceptions of the world. He's been firmly
committed to developing my critical thinking skills by focusing
on the importance of process, and is always seeking ways to push
my work further and cultivate the way I think about my work.
He is particularly focused on integrating my past experiences
and expertise in non-design areas, including residence life,
project management, and Liberal Arts, into my design process.
His mentorship has had a huge influence on the way I think
about design and the way I approach my own work and his
uncompromising commitment to myself and my peers has been
an integral part of my development as a designer.

  – Eva Schipper

It takes years of practice to be a good designer, the effort of becoming a good teacher grows exponentially. I did my design program at Emily Carr University of Art and Design and had the pleasure to meet and study from Thomas. We all know creativity doesn't just come from memorization, great designers have great empathy and can feel the world. Thomas's class has always been the one that bring out our personality and creativity, he didn't just tell us the rules and the principles in design, but rather he used a variety of approaches to inspire us and guide us to explore. I now worked as a UX/UI designer at Conquer Mobile, and what I have learnt from his classes certainly got me very prepared, and more importantly, very excited for entering the industry.

– Desmond Gao

Thomas has done everything in his power to assist me in reaching my goal of becoming a professional user-experience designer. He's made himself available to meet for coffee, he sends timely emails and he also encouraging me be better on a daily basis. Over the years, he has helped me and many other students to flourish, by teaching us to network and he also has amazing insights which have brought our design projects and resume to a really good place. Under his guidance, I've had the privilege of meeting with talented designers working at Mozilla Firefox, Ayogo and Domain 7. The guy just wants to help his students and the satisfaction of seeing us succeed in life is why he's put in so much of his time.

– Ryan McKay

First of all, I really appreciate Thomas taught me something new and useful about design and art stuff in the ECU program about

UI/UX + App + web knowledge. Thomas' classes are like good tea or good wine, you may not taste the difference at the very first but the great taste will come out after a second. Honestly, I didn't understand the importance of card sorting and mood board in the first 2 weeks. When the courses in the program had more and more design decisions to make, those new skills were very useful. More than just brainstorming, card sorting helped to choose the better paths for many projects. Basically, the skill reroutes the way I think not only about design but also about my photography work. I miss Thomas' Monday morning class in the Summer.

— Raymond Leung

2

GRATITUDE 2: ABSTRACTS

Accepted Abstract at the Seventeenth International Conference on the Arts in Society, 2022 on Advanced Typography Workshops in Quarantine

The argument is always that design isn't about saving lives. Some people argue for its importance, for example with the historical example of poorly-designed election ballots causing American voters to be confused enough to vote for the wrong party or candidate. Teaching typography during the pandemic puts an interesting lens on it. In one sense it is the least of our worries, but historically it has been so important that it must not be allowed to gather dust.

Accepted Abstract at the Sixteenth International Conference on the Arts in Society, 2021 on Unique Ways of Making

I currently run this offering in Oculus VR (social online reality) environment "Altspace". The process of making is not hard to figure out. Choosing actionable items towards what constitutes "making" is hard. In this workshop, you'll be introduced to some surprising, easy, and effective ways of prototyping which I've taught at Emily Carr University of Art and Design. We will go through different fidelities of making using everything from a roll of masking tape to a blindfold fabric. Then, for the workshop option, you'll have a chance to attempt at making with a partner. We will use a process called role play which requires no knowledge, no creative ability, just a desire to learn and be inspired.

Accepted Abstract at the Fifteenth International Conference on Design Principles & Practices, 2021 on Unique Ways of Prototyping

The process of prototyping is not hard to figure out. Choosing actionable items towards what constitutes "prototyping" is hard. In this workshop, you'll be introduced to some surprising, easy, and effective ways of prototyping which I've taught at Emily Carr University of Art and Design. We will go through different fidelities of prototyping using everything from a roll of masking tape to a blindfold fabric. Then, for the workshop option, you'll have a chance to attempt at prototyping with a partner. We will use a process called role play which requires no knowledge, no creative ability, just a desire to learn and be inspired.

Accepted Abstract at the Fourteenth International Conference on Design Principles & Practices, 2020 on The A4 Workshop

This session considers a project about rapid conceptualization and realization through sketches and reference material. The conceptualization for this project originated from historical project ideas that were taught at the Bauhaus. In this project, students have one hour and one piece of A4 size paper to make something. The students can make whatever they want and are not given further direction beyond a brief introduction. Some of the hour students have is allocated by the student to decide what a story might be that they could tell around what they have. A timer is set to emphasize the significance of time and the use of time in the project. After the hour is over there is a critique session, where dialogue begins around stories the student have created about what they've made, thinking in terms of a way to introduce themselves and create discussion around design, as a segue into further studies and projects.

Accepted Abstract at the Fifteenth International Conference on The Arts in Society, 2020 on Unique Ways of Prototyping

This workshop is built around a method called role play, which uses voice and writing to make, test, and iterate an idea. Participants are first paired up and assigned roles. One person represents a user, and one person represents a product or service that will be interrogated by that user. As a jumping off point, we might say that the product or service is a voice user interface like Siri. Once the roles are assigned to the the pairs, they have a conversation based on their roles; in this case, a conversation between Siri, and a person using Siri. This often happens for a timed interval of ten minutes. After the ten minutes is up, the second half of the workshop begins. In the same pairs, the same conversation happens except this time, we focus on variations of the product or service. The workshop concludes with a takeaway idea. Next time, try this process instead of in pairs, in a group of three, where the third person is a note taker who just listens to the interactive conversation between the pair and turns it into writing. In addition to voice user interfaces, this can easily be adapted to interrogate the relationship between users and mobile devices, or within more pioneering technologies like VR and AR.

Accepted Abstract at the Fourteenth International Conference on the Arts in Society, 2019 on One Hundred Watch Faces

This project is about rapid conceptualization and realization through sketches and reference material. Considering that we often as designers believe that we must spend time on something and get it right, this exercise is being given. I've given the same exercise in Shanghai while teaching at a design school there. The reality is we are in a time when maybe the most important aspect of the creative process is quickly making something to get it in front of someone. This idea of "the maker" is something that often spurs discussion in interaction design circles, but can be applied to any specialization. Recently "design thinking" has come to the forefront, which might be recognized looking at walls full of post-it notes using processes with complex names like affinity diagramming, card sorting and paper prototyping. In reality the process is cyclical, moving from concept, to making, to testing, over and over as quickly as possible. We work to pull out mistakes which can be critiqued and modified through a next iteration. The simplicity of the project, looking at existing watches and drawing them, one hundred of them, is reductionist. The project is in fact a process of quickly bringing an idea into a manifestation of that idea through sketching, then quickly making another sketch as a result of having made the first sketch.

Accepted Abstract at the Thirteenth International Conference on Design Principles & Practices, 2019 on The Helvetica Project

Based on the idea that designing a logotype without a fundamental knowledge of typography is too ambitious a concept, this project came about. Starting with Helvetica Neue in one weight, either bold, light, or ultra light, we will build a word mark in this session. A work mark might be described as a word typeset in one size and weight of a typeface, with a slight modification to one of the glyphs. One might change the axis of the bowl, or change the length of one of the ascenders or descenders, of create something slightly more illustrative. Ideally the modification made will allow the word to communicate in a new way, visually and perhaps metaphorically. But the important part is that the modification to a glyph is a small change, making the mark only slightly different from the Helvetica typesetting itself. The result will be a word mark which is a modified version of the ubiquitous Helvetica Neue, which can act to build identity for a project, concept, or idea. One might call it a logotype, and they may be correct, however the project is given as something that is achievable within a shorter timeframe and maybe helps a student to begin to appreciate typographic anatomy like bowls, stems, ascenders, and other glyphs.

3

GRATITUDE 3: LITERARY JOURNAL ESSAYS

Advanced Typography Workshops in Quarantine: Published Text in The Ormsby Review, Graduate Liberal Studies Journal, 2021

Saving Lives

The argument is always that design isn't about saving lives. Some people argue for its importance, for example with the historical example of poorly-designed election ballots causing American voters to be confused enough to vote for the wrong party or candidate. Teaching typography during the pandemic puts an interesting lens on it. In one sense it is the least of our worries, but historically it has been so important that it must not be allowed to gather dust. I teach a class called Advanced Typography at a small private design school in Vancouver and I often reflect on how, throughout history, typography has been carefully documented and considered in practical ways in its relationship with current technologies, in the impact it has on people emotionally and, most importantly, in the way we read. Letters are meant to be read, and through the careful study of topics like typographic readability and legibility we can assess its continuing importance. Some say we can never see history while it's unfolding, but I simply offer this précis of typographic studies so that perhaps we can reflect, "Wait a minute, writing actually says a lot."

The Poster

The poster is the hallmark of typography, the one deliverable that will never disappear. It had its heyday during the Grunge period when cool bands plastered printed posters all over the place, and any designer could make a decent living designing and typesetting these. At some point that shifted and we had to ask ourselves if we had to repurpose posters, thinking of them as a little square Instagram icon on the corner of a screen, or on the side of a Greyhound bus, or in between YouTube videos before the person watching hits the skip button. Or as a motion graphics trailer before a feature film. The question of the relevance of a poster will of course never be fully valid simply because it has so much good baggage. It's what designers knew and loved and learnt about growing up, and this will continue to be true for as long as knowledge gets passed along. And yes, in a school where we design for screens and try to be vocational to match the needs of industry today, we have to ask ourselves if posters will make the cut into curriculum. I can promise you one thing: those with wisdom will ensure they will.

Dinner Table Conversation

As design becomes dinner table conversation I hope that typography makes the cut – so that people can laugh about
Comic Sans, or chuckle about Helvetica at a defunct American
Apparel clothing store. It's funny to me that American Apparel
is now history and no longer current. I suppose that's what
happens as time marches forward – your own history continues
to be relevant to you and casts a magic spell that makes you
smile when you see typographic instructions for a VCR, or the
typography of a novel falling apart at the seams in a thrift
shop. My focus on the history of design at this time might
seem questionable, but admit that I enjoy talking about the
Bauhaus, and the time when sans serifs were emerging, and the
time of the chopping off of the serifs, as some designers refer
to it during that period; and the illuminated manuscripts that
included letters hand-drawn by scribes before the proliferation
of the printing press, or the wicked angularity of type during
Russian Constructivism. But these are tangential these days.
They are in some ways specifically typographic matters.

London

I had a trip to London somewhat recently and became overjoyed
when I found a Josef Albers original in a small frame around
a less-looked-at corner of the Tate Modern. In my course I
talk about Albers and Itten for their contributions to colour
theory during the Bauhaus. A quick aside: typographic colour
is actually a grey colour, which we perceive when we look at a
page filled with letters and squint our eyes. Of course, we can
open Photoshop and select a letter and pick a red swatch, and
the colour will change; and I still feel deflated when asked to
convince a group of young designers that colour is not in fact

colour as we know it, when they just want to use the Pantone Colour of the Year, or when they have never used anything other than Twitter Blue. Who am I to say? These days the authoritative knowledge of an instructor can be questioned like anything else, and sometimes it makes me wonder what relevance I have other than facilitating critiques and telling stories, the odd one that we can all chuckle at. But I guess that is a legitimate role, and perhaps most academics will agree that the life of an academic has plenty of paradox. Paradoxes? Often I wish I was young enough again to simply be an adult's curiosity.

Motion Graphics

When asked to talk about motion graphics I still mention a design production studio that was already history 15 years ago when a professor introduced it to me. Imaginary Forces during its heyday did all the big typographic Hollywood blockbuster trailers, or at least the coolest ones, based out of a little studio in LA. I Googled them to see if they are still around. They are, and they're now doing perhaps the less desirable of those blockbusters, but, I imagine, as profitable as ever. Students have no idea about references that are second nature to me, so I feel sometimes that I transmit information that students will actually read and enjoy and remember, which is a nice feeling. They should read from the reading list (see Works Cited, below), but they complain it's too expensive. I tell them they only need to buy one book, offering A History of Graphic Design, by Alston Purvis and Philip Meggs, for its high-quality reproductions of movie posters and posters for bands. But you can't tell young people anything these days. They might agree or argue, but they will move on to the next thing pretty quickly without much care for what came before it.

Grids

Grids can be taught right at the beginning, but that's not how I learned about them. I was taught to experiment first. Only later did I learn that typography had been organized very carefully so that it made sense. Typography really made sense with connected terms like The Swiss Style, The International Typographic Style, and Modernism, and it wasn't hard to prove that even Postmodernism and simple chaos made sense. Still, when I look at a layout with timeless typography, I do feel it's better, but perhaps that's just the bias of an aging designer. Grids are in a handful of things that I teach right at the beginning. Names like Josef Muller Brockmann are connected to those times that witnessed the transitions between Modernism and Postmodernism, making for a rule-based world in contrast to running around like chickens without their heads.

Negative Space

One thing I'll say about negative space is that I have typography students who really like to fill up all the space with everything. If they are reading this they should know this is not an original endeavour. The space that's filled or black and the space that's empty or white work in tandem, with some saying the white negative is where the DNA is – it's what we read. I call this filling up of space decorative design simply to make a point, not as a subtle way of insulting something I don't fully understand. And one could fight back claiming that to leave a page blank is no better. What I do know is that elements work together and somehow rub off on each other, in the process tainting our perception of a page. Typography is an art and a science. The practised specialist uses negative space to guide the eye, lead us around shapes that affect our memory and subconscious, and determines how we read, even through the negative.

Clarity

So, the next obvious idea would be that typography should be clear and it should be readable. No different than written words, one might claim, as William Zinsser asserts in On Writing Well. Instead of overpowering, typography should recede and weave its magic without intruding or butting in with showy stylization. It should cast and retain its spell after the dust has settled. Type that shouts is in opposition to this, but type that whispers might also draw attention to itself and for that reason could be equally unnecessary. Helvetica, the font, was always the emblem of transparency, but history taints itself, and in current times Helvetica printed and posted on an out-of-service bathroom door, or on a no smoking sign might say a little too much too soon. So even clarity in typography is riddled with complexity as it struggles to free itself. In short, typography needs a day off once in a while too.

Mathematics

Mathematics and typography are not distant cousins. Mathematical patterns seen in the proportions of a human body, in the shell of a snail, and in the ripples of the ocean if we stretch a little, are just as much typographic as they are parts of nature. The Fibonacci series is one example of this: a series of numbers from nature that can work to create harmonious design. In traditional design education, words like beauty, elegance, and timelessness have always been synonymous with good design. We now live in a design world where things have to be tested and evaluated before they can ring true, but believers in human-centred design and more universal aesthetics might still draw on mathematics to communicate, and they would be perfectly correct. Break a page into three equal parts, and you have a "rule of thirds" layout which still stands tall as a soldier marching for math and typography. The curious craftsman who ignores the three sections, well, they are just as susceptible to its genetic order. And when a radical designer makes a jumbled mess, let's just say that it also has its place.

Contrast

Contrast in typography is another magic trick. How do you make contrast? Look closely first. Even a blank page is something, and its proportions are something to contrast it with. Add an element to the page, some letters for example, and you might begin to imagine the complexity that even a lazy detective would find, balancing proportions with negative space and an inked surface. And then do less. Doing less is hard work. Two patient competitors both doing less might be the cause of the most vicious battle, doing nothing at all while also doing everything, all at the same time. In other words, even in silence there is white noise, and if a tree falls in the woods there is always a tree falling, and in the blackness of night there is the blackest black. We are always in the elements. This is typographic contrast.

An Alarming Fact

If you told me an alarming fact that people spend their whole lives designing fonts, I might think you are telling me a joke I didn't understand. In fact, the design of letters has been going on for a very long time. The first examples in our recorded history are inscriptions on tablets recording ownership of land and other financials, while equally early on are the illuminated manuscripts – labour-intensive and valuable hand-lettered books that, at the time, were equivalent of owning a house today. And when the printing press emerged, people interned carving type out of lead. They might never complete more than one letter a day. Type has existed in all shapes throughout history, and always behind it all were type designers. These days, with a computer, it's faster but not better, even though type designers today are capable and what they create is good. People like Matthew Carter, known for working at Microsoft Typography on faces like Verdana and Georgia, have made letters in virtually all the ways they've ever been made, in contrast to type designers today or in the recent past who might find themselves with a pirated copy of fontlab and some curiosity. In the documentary Helvetica, Matthew Carter argues that it's very difficult to sit on a plane or a train these days and answer when someone asks what you do and you answer type designer. They might reply, "I thought they were all dead."

Vocabulary

Kerning, letter-spacing, counters, and ascenders and descenders are all part of this mystery system we call typographic vocabulary. Much like Canadians might learn to speak both English and French, a designer during their formal education might be forced to learn the language of English along with the language

35

of typography, a highly visual form of the English language that traditionally helped copyrighters communicate with art directors in ad agencies or in editorial design. The markings on a page using these words is one way that designers communicated with one another through annotation. However, in most Adobe Software we can quickly change some aspects of typography in a vector software like InDesign or a more common program, Adobe Illustrator. But more importantly, through typographic vocabulary, we can talk about those changes and only afterwards make changes that might make or break typography.

Arms and Legs

Much like we have arms and legs, typefaces have anatomy. Alexander Lawson's book The Anatomy of a Typeface was evidence of this, solidifying the idea that the anatomy of a typeface was real while finding a place on every typographer's bookshelf, if only to be read by the title on its spine. Much like we have a stomach that can be round and empty sometimes, the lowercase o also has an empty stomach, the negative space inside the letter, a counter. Little feet are called serifs. Type with long arms and legs might be considered to have ascenders and descenders. Some wording for typographic anatomy is very ordinary, like typography with feet or typography with arms or legs. A letter might wear a hat, or it might look like a water droplet called a teardrop serif. Other letters that look like binoculars like a g we simply call a binocular g. All of these words describing the anatomy of type slowly cast a magic spell and let us see the world a little differently. Erik Spiekermann in Stop Stealing Sheep and Find Out How Type Works talks about how he enjoys looking at letters while some people enjoy looking at, ahem, nude women or men. Letters are his friends, he says.

Best Practices

We need to discuss certain recommendations. Never stretch type, for a type designer may have spent years of their life making the thing, and then to turn it into a deformity in a matter of seconds is horrific. Never use Comic Sans except perhaps for a comic book, since a comic book is what it was designed for. Every font has a purpose. Use it for that. Most of the time the side of a truck isn't meant to look like a comic book, so why would you make it look that way? Comic Sans has a bad reputation beyond this, as something cited to avoid, but I don't see it that way. Instead it's something we should carefully consider and employ for its intended use, which I'll admit is very limited in scope, and which puts it in a corner by itself most of the time. Putting generous amounts of space between capital letters, also known as letter-spacing, is usually good, as capital letters are notoriously hard to read in longer strings of text, and this letter-spacing will help it. On the other hand, tightening the letter-spacing in a font like Helvetica can actually help Helvetica, as we read word shapes; so when there is less space between characters in certain fonts with upper and lower case, reducing the negative space helps us understand it as our eyes travel over the shapes and as we engage in the process of reading. Of course there are exceptions. Spekiermann says you shouldn't put too much space between lowercase letters. People understood it and learnt that, but then they disagreed and did exactly what he said not to do. They rejected an idea once learnt, which is of course is another way.

Climate

In our current typographic climate I am often called on to talk about the type of the present day. Which font should I use? Should I pay for a font? How can I learn about type? I wish I could offer shortcuts, but there aren't many. Today type has to work on the small screens of our iPhones, or it has to move around a screen in video, which affects the job of a type designer as well as the job of a typographer. Old type that hasn't been digitized recently often suffers in small-screen environments. Google fonts is an alternative. But is it complete? Type today considers a myriad of modalities that we never could have imagined ten or five years ago. To make it relevant today we have to look at it in these new contexts and ask ourselves if it is still relevant; we have to think about how we can amplify the value of a craft that has been invested in so heavily over time, we must admit it will hold an important place in history. We are the key decision makers for our future.

What do you imagine?

References

- Gary Hustwit, Shelby Siegel, and Luke Geissbuhler, Helvetica: A Documentary Film (Plexifilm, 2007).
- Thomas King, The Truth About Stories: A Native Narrative (Toronto: House of Anansi Press, 2003).
- AlexanderLawson,TheAnatomyofaTypeface(DavidR.Godine ,1990).
- Alston W. Purvis and Philip B. Meggs, A History of Graphic

Design (2006).
- Eric Spiekermann, Stop Stealing Sheep and Find Out How Type Works (Peachpit Press, 2014).
- William Zinsser, On Writing Well: An Informal Guide to Writing Nonfiction (New York: Harper Collins,

1990).

Dear Thomas King: Published Text in The Ormsby Review, Graduate Liberal Studies Journal, 2020

Dear Thomas King,

Pandemic. I live in a room. In the room there are objects. And by way of you, the objects have stories. We all know objects to have stories. We choose them, buy them, include them in our lives, and continue to include them or discard them. They are a part of us. And the reasons behind them are also a part of us.

These days I think about the stories of innocuous things. Things that you wouldn't think have stories.

At Emily Carr University of Art and Design, in some down time, I had a chance to visit the house of a faculty member who taught a course called "Art Direction." "Art Direction" in this context was about objects and their stories, and the faculty member informed us that everything in her house had a story. She told us the stories as we walked through the house, and in disbelief, we learned that it was true.

Today I'm flanked by objects and their stories. From a Patagonia jacket that makes me think of life in the Bay Area, to a Manzini book that reminds me of pan-con-to-mate in Barcelona, to New Balance sneakers that remind me of my first contract design job, to an Apple mouse that reminds me of dark patterns.

As you note about just about any story, "Take it. You've heard it... it's yours now."[1]

References

- [1] From Thomas King, The Truth About Stories: A Native Narrative (Toronto: Anansi, 2003) (CBC Massey Lectures Series)

Unique ways of prototyping: Published Text in The Ormsby Review, Graduate Liberal Studies Journal, 2020

When I talk about "prototyping" here, I'm talking about it in part as I've learnt it in traditional design education, at Emily Carr University of Art + Design, years ago. In that realm we broke down the processes of designing into a number of steps, and prototyping was one of them.

Basically, when designers envision and agree on a product to make, they need to make an example first. If it was the design of a shoe, that prototype might be that exact shoe carved and milled out of balsa wood and foam core, not for making lots of, but as a single sample. If it was a website, the prototype might be a picture. Not a working version, not clickable, not accessible through a browser, but instead a sample picture for presentation. It might be seen as a bit of a trick, if you think it's the real thing.

The iconic historical example of this trick is when Steve Jobs presented the Next Computer to a broad audience in a lecture hall in 1988. He actually hadn't readied the Next for distribution, it was simply a single copy that was good enough to use for presentation. In that context everyone thought it was done. Arguably he fooled the audience into thinking they could buy these on the shelves when there was actually only one in existence, the prototype.

Introduction

Plato inspired me to frame and write about my own speaking in terms of classical rhetorical theory.[1] I contextualize my discussion of my design talks within the more positive ideas of Plato's student Aristotle, first touching on his three fundamental laws of logic (ethos, pathos, logos),[2] then I move to Cicero and his five canons (inventio, dispositio, elocutio, memoria, actio). Although these are of less interest to me than coming to terms with Plato's struggle with the morals of rhetoric, they end up being wild areas of exploration and appreciation of the sort of work I am doing in my design workshops and lectures. I organize my narrative according to conventions of rhetorical practice, and in my sub-headings I establish the various sections as elements of a rhetorical discourse. In this way, classical rhetorical theory adds value to what might otherwise be a narrative pastiche.

Late in 2019, by invitation I gave a talk at Vancouver tech staple Mobify titled "Unique Ways of Prototyping." Already nervous, after months of anticipation, I buzzed the organizer to take me up the elevators of the Microsoft building on Burrard. No one was there yet, but very soon people here and there started to shuffle about, unfolding scissor chairs and propping up floor banners. One of them danced with questions. "How do you want these chairs set-up?" It was my first prompt. "Can you leave them separated slightly? — I need it that way for the workshop portion," I replied. One of them asked, "Like this?" I nodded.

It was already starting to happen. I placed my bottled water by the podium, a trick of the trade to calm nerves and provide a break in the middle of my talk. This was a talk now. This was something different. I had been a lecturer before. I knew the binaries — the audience's role, the speaker's role — but this was something different.

Let me start with a big reveal. I will say the punch line is that you can teach digital tools and processes with nothing but voice, nothing but a conversation. A conversation is making. A conversation is prototyping. Let me explain by talking about writing, and how writing is, in fact, making. For how ideas flow from your imagination into the real world through writing, as they appear on an inked surface... your ideas are manifesting themselves. In this way, a manifestation of ideas happens. Writing is also prototyping.

A second slide shows three people in conversation. Here, making is happening as well, this time through voice and more complexity. As a person conveys their ideas, the ideas leave the imagination and become part of the world. They become part of the world sonically. They become part of the world through sound and conversation, and through the conversation the ideas adapt and evolve. This is also prototyping.

And finally, a slide is shown of a round table discussion, where among ten actors, ideas are manifesting through voice, through sound, and through writing, and through a lot of activity. The latter half of the talk concerns how these processes can be used to make digital things. And how at Emily Carr University of Art + Design this is what we do, we make digital things. However, in this entire presentation about prototyping, we never show a computer. We never show an iPhone, an interface, an input/output device. Instead, it's all analog. which is a fancy way of saying that there actually isn't any substance here at all.

Ethos

One of Aristotle's modes of persuasion, ethos, appears in a couple of instances during this talk. I will assume a basic knowledge of ethos and rhetoric, as for the purpose of the paper I am only able to note these instances as I reflect on the talks. Through my Mobify talk I'm quick to mention a couple of facts that don't really tie to the illustration of my journey through "Unique ways of prototyping" at all, and so upon reflection I asked myself why they landed so well, and why I included them. Was it gaudy to include them?

This presentation was somewhat improvised, so I was reading the room in deciding what to say. And two improvised "ethos" things I rely on are my TEDx talk and my Assistant Professor posting in India. As I have come to understand myself better through this writing, I now see these improvisations as Aristotelian persuasive strategies. For example, I mentioned the TEDx talk, even though it is irrelevant to the communication of my personal journey, as well as my linear narrative through the slides. However, when a slide comes up I'm quick to mention, "This is me at my recent TEDx talk." It consistently grabs attention right away. The second, and the point I open the slides with, is my work as an assistant professor in India. It's irrelevant in communicating anything about "Unique ways of prototyping," but it feels right and helps paint a picture of me. You could say that I employ these two experiences try to captivate the audience by building credibility. When people hear these two things, they listen, and they say to themselves "I should listen because he knows something."

Penn State

Late in 2018, by invitation, I gave a talk titled "Vulnerability" at Land Grant Institution Pennsylvania State University, at their Stuckeman School in State College, Pennsylvania.

Arriving at Stuckeman School after a good night's sleep was very pleasant. This beautifully architected space supports an interior architecture program, which, after taking the tour, I thought was simply amazing. They asked, "Do you have research interests?" I was silent. "We have large budgets for research, like all the land grant institutions here. Here, let me take you for the tour." I was paraded around a beautiful open-plan space surrounded by greenery, in some ways resembling Emily Carr, that provides a space for speaking. "We have a lot of complaints about this space because the speakers' voices echo into the halls, so it makes recording talks difficult. The tech will come meet you and mic you up after you meet a few people this morning."

I had a good feeling about the talk. The work of my past student, Amy, in prototyping using a blindfold fabric was so basic and I thought they would love it. I explained how we could build empathy for visually impaired users with her idea. A person with correct vision puts on the blindfold and sees like a visually impaired user. Her project restored circadian rhythms in visually impaired users by introducing good habits that don't depend on vision.

I kept returning to a focus on people instead of technology, presenting case study after case study about how we were doing amazing things at Emily Carr that take the dependence on technology out of technology related projects. We now design by understanding people's wants and needs. I showed another slide of rough drawings on index cards of what a related mobile application might look like.

Finally, talking about digital, I introduced the Raspberry Pi, a credit card sized computer that is used in teaching and en-trepreneurship. I explained the possibilities of prototyping with the thing. And how easy it was to learn. Time wound down and I ended the presentation abruptly as my iPhone timer went off. "Questions?"

Pathos

In retrospect, my attempt to employ Aristotle's pathos, a mode of persuasion focused on desire to trust a person, was a mistake. My ideas were overly ambitious for the audience and my abrupt ending made the presentation seem half-baked. I did not address common sense ideas that would help the audience feel they could easily "get it," and it showed. Only two people came up to me afterwards. I had failed at persuasion. Of course, at the time I didn't know it, but later it seemed obvious. The clothing I was wearing, crumpled from my suitcase, didn't help with pathos. My unshaven look didn't help with pathos. And the kicker, the sonically-unfriendly speaking space, hurt pathos. But anyway, my story continues.

TEDx

In early 2019, I gave a TEDx talk. The theme was "Greater than you" and the venue was Reliance Theatre at Emily Carr University of Art + Design.

I sat down with Emily Carr University faculty member Scott Mallory, Jr. He was wearing a black ball cap and a black and red lanyard that repeated TEDxECUAD over and over. His brown skin surprised me. "I don't know if you really want to do this." He was already trying to turn me away. He went into a speech. Finally, he asked me what my "idea worth sharing" was, which I hadn't even thought about. "Spending time in airports," I blurted out. "Bwa ha ha ha! I can relate to that," Scott said. He continued, explaining. "You would be a backup. You can come for the rehearsals though." That was February 2019.

And from there I would arrive at Reliance Theatre every Saturday. I perched my iPhone against a wall on video recording mode. I wanted to see myself. Sometimes I would even go during weekdays. The theatre was empty and I would recite to an empty room. "Another dropped," said Scott. "That's four drops. I'll confirm you over the next day or so." The minutes felt like hours as I awaited that confirmation. Nothing came through. I messaged Scott. "Yeah, yeah, you are confirmed. A bunch of people dropped. You'll be the only faculty." A formal email came through. I was speaking at a TED.

"For as long as I can remember, I wanted to travel all around the world," my voice echoed, "but it turns out my favourite places to be are the airports. I realized this was true when I found myself boarding a plane to Seattle just to visit their airport." Scott laughed.

We were in final rehearsals and I decided not to wear shoes. Somehow it felt right without shoes. The talk was about that comfort. About craving things that are familiar. About craving things that feel like home. Scott had changed the order of some phrases around at the last minute in my script. "Another time I was on my way to Barcelona and I was dreaming about Barcelona things." I recalled that trip to Barcelona where I received an emerging scholar award, and tried to make it relatable. "Eating Pan con Tomate, sipping a Tempranillo." The audience laughed. I could feel their warmth.

"It's different now!" said Scott. "But we can work with it." I tried to tune Scott out. Everything went dark. The intonation of my voice changed:

So, next time you are on a plane, think about some of these things. The Diet Coke, tomato
    juice, Christmas, two-ply toilet paper, seat belts ... even think about Hollywood movies. And think about how these things might remind you of home. Maybe you'll find yourself on a plane too. Just to visit: an airport.

I waved to the audience as I walked off stage.

Logos

Viewed through the lens of Aristotle's Logos, it now makes sense how I pushed this talk through. I pushed this talk to be accepted. It probably started when I realized that my talk idea was exactly what Scott wanted. I reasoned at every angle how it was for Scott: how it was about travelling a lot, which Scott did. It was about always being in airports, which Scott often was. It was about helping solve the problem of being short on speakers, which Scott had as well. And my talk was safe. After Scott did the ghost writing of the first paragraph of the talk, I memorized it word for word and recited it that way too. It was exactly what Scott wanted. Scott is a reasonable person and by my reasonable measure, this talk was making it in. The appeal to the audience would also be decided by Scott: the cadence, the segues, the gestures. the timing. Scott's vision was clear and I was going to follow it. This was a talk based on reason.

In Oculus VR [VR = virtual reality] environment "Altspace," I'm asked to host "Unique Ways of Making" every Friday from 4:00 PM to 5:00 PM (PST).

"The future is now." A comment came through in WhatsApp. Microsoft had just acquired Altspace, and there was a lot of excitement around VR. Yunji — that's her avatar name — who works at Microsoft Altspace had walked me through how to run a VR event in Altspace. "If someone opens a portal, just open the host panel and you can kick them. You can ban them here."

I've been putting on my Oculus VR goggles to enter Altspace, checking out the stage, pulling up my slide deck in VR. It's probably one of the biggest venues I've presented in, as the stage feels like it commands attention, the upper level and outdoor balcony provide unique views of the stage, and a nice place to mingle afterwards with the vehicle traffic noise in the background. There is plentiful capacity for a good-sized audience. The catch? None of its real. Or rather, it's all in virtual reality.

Dorothy986 (her handle) and I became friends in Altspace, and she agreed to moderate the event. I muted the audience. With my Oculus headset half on, so I could still press the forward key for the slides from my keyboard, I began speaking. It was mostly the same as a talk I had given before, but I could tell that I was grabbing the audience's attention, which is more or less an impossibility in VR.

"Can I get some heart and clap emojis?" Heart shaped red icons streamed above the avatars' heads in the audience. "Okay once more in a selfie this time! Wait — my eyes were closed. Once more. Okay, awesome! Awesome!" It was awesome. "Writing is making. And talking — conversation is making, you know that now...." Dorothy986 kicked a couple of people "And here we have a group of people in a round table discussion, so complexity, complexity in the making. I'll round out the slide deck with a class I've taught at Emily Carr and then we will go into the workshop." I was excited. New Age stuff! That's what my aunt calls it. I told her it's actually not that new anymore.

Plato would agree. This was his apprehensive rhetoric. My audience was filled with secondary school kids whose classes were cancelled due to the Coronavirus. Others were friends of friends. These were masses waiting to be convinced. Waiting,

49

waiting, and ready to believe what I had to say, as long as I put a little gloss on it. Massaged it a bit. This was not the kind of public speaking I enjoyed, because it didn't require any effort to try to be authentic to land well. To try to reach people; to try to connect. All that structure had already been established. And so my well-intended talk, my well received talk, fell flat in my mind. But in the audience's mind it worked wonderfully. And afterwards my talk would be praised. Like a Plato rhetorician, focused on a talk divorced from content, it convinced anyway despite its VR deception and untruth.

Unique Ways of Prototyping for Idea Validation

In February 2020, I gave a talk to Mobify in the Microsoft building in Vancouver to attendees. "Unique Ways of Prototyping for Idea Validation" was something new.

I stood as attendees arrived. Some nice teamwork pulling chairs off the hooks for 83 attendees fell short, and some would be standing or sitting on the couches in the back. This was a big audience for me, but I did not feel the nerves. Organizer Dilan Ustek had brought in her whole network of meet- up.com researchers to watch me speak about research, an area I would love to learn more about. An area I knew little about. But I wasn't nervous, I was this content and this content was me. I knew it well. I lived it and that's how I would present it.

Microsoft had done an amazing job taking a spot in this skyscraper where I would give my talk. Glad to be back; I was ready. Mingling and pizza turned into a rush of people for the seats, but the number was perfect. For a pay-to-attend talk, just the right number showed up. And I was ready: ready to be vulnerable. Ready to be relatable. Ready to be interactive. I pulled up the slides on the MacBook Pro for a last glance, a nice professional photo of myself stared back at me. "Thomas Girard" it said. "That's me. I am Thomas Girard."

"And this..." A long breath followed and I was having trouble speaking. "...is at TEDx after I had given my talk. Three of us are in conversation here." Something was happening with my speech, I could not finish a sentence without taking a breath in between. Fear of public speaking: nothing new. Quirky Thomas Girard. Nothing new. They all know you are quirky. "And that conversation is making."

I landed that vocal full stop and felt my confidence come back. I was in it again. And then my mic died. Almost simpatico a volunteer passed a back-up to me, and then offered to forward the slides on my MacBook Pro keyboard for me. Supporters, so nice to have support. Everything would be smooth from then on.

"So, any Oculus users?" I asked. "Just one? That's so bad!" The audience laughed in tandem. "Okay, for the workshop portion one of you is the Oculus and one of you is the user of Oculus. I'm going to set a timer for ten minutes for you all. Ready?" They burst into conversation with each other. I grabbed my mug of water and took a sip, and just watched and eavesdropped. I made this! I made this happen. I was beaming. I paced around the stage a bit and checked the timer a few times. I looked at the volunteers and they looked back at me wide-eyed, as if they were asking me how I did it. I did it. It was happening.

Plato

Plato would have seen this, in his early ideas about the formality of rhetoric, as a good example of his kind of rhetoric. This was my third time at Mobify as a speaker. I started losing track of what was coming out of my mouth; as an orator I was just vocalizing. The rhetoric that has nothing to do with the content. A decorated, embellished blob.

Suburbs

In 2019 I gave a "Unique Ways of Making Things" talk-workshop at Richmond's Culture Days, to an audience of 3. My dad, Greg Girard, was one of those in the audience. "You should charge," he professed. "Greg, I think we have different ideologies," I replied. I ended the email thread there. Again, more of the same from my dad. The truth is I was happy to be included in the Minoru Precinct at Richmond Culture Days. I really did feel like it was a big win for me to have that space. It was the start of something. Besides, I just wanted to spread my ideas.

"So, it's 80 dollars to use the projector for the day." "Okay," I replied. Thank goodness my dad wasn't there yet. Three people showed up. Cleveland Stordy was one, a friend who agreed to be a videographer, and another was my dad. The two of them sat in the back of the room chatting. "I'll do a second running of the talk in about 15 minutes," I asked. Can you tell people?" I was competing against a popular workshop next door in the auditorium, the main event there. My dad left after the first presentation and I gave an intimate presentation to a couple who

52

came in and mainly wanted to do the workshop. They thanked me and said how great it was. I was happy. Cleveland stayed to the end. I wanted to repay him. "Beer and pizza?"

A kid and her parent and a couple of seniors sat at the boardroom table. "So, I'm super glad to be here at Richmond Culture Days! There are so many great events going on right now and I feel privileged to be a part of it!" I did feel privilege. But I was talking to an audience of five people. And I was nervous. As I progressed I got into the swing of it. "This is the first time I've run this event as 'Unique Ways of Making Things.' Ordinarily I run it as 'Unique Ways of Prototyping.'"

I had only run it a couple of times. I faulted myself for my lack of authenticity. "Questions?" Then conversation filled the room like a warm blanket. These people, sparse as they may be, had been touched. They told others to come and watch and stay. They felt it was something special. And they stayed. They stayed to ask questions. I could run this again. I would run this again.

Inventio

I started with a blank browser tab. I started typing in queries. Vancouver. Call for speakers. Nothing came up. This was my inventio phase. To find or discover. The bing of an email notified me of another email. Subject: Richmond Culture Days. Hm, that might work. Here I was coming up with an idea. I thought back to my friend, Stephanie Ostler, a TEDx speaker, who, early in her career, worked the craft fair scene selling women's lingerie, which wasn't that much different. Compose. "I'm interested in running a workshop at your event.... Thanks in advance."

Send.

Bangalore

A roundtable discussion in Bangalore, at India's UX [UX = user experience] conference by way of appointment as Assistant Professor at a university near Mumbai, 2018.

We don't have a ticket. Fuck. Get Ashish on the phone. "We've flown in from Ajeenkya DY Patil University." I watched as that very phone call turned our presence from odd suspicion to miraculous welcome. "So, we don't have a lanyard for you — just write your name on here."

It was a packed hotel. I had no idea there were so many designers in Bangalore. I checked my phone again. "We would like to invite you to be part of a round table panel discussion for design heads." My luck was turning. "We would also like to invite you to be part of a round table panel discussion for design educators."

I entered the little room and once again was startled by how nice it was, and how ugly it was outside, the huge division between those who are included in these sorts of things and those who are not.

"Stay." I told my student from Ajeenkya DY Patil University who was chaperoning me, as the professor, around the conference. "No, the invitation was for you..." "Let's get a coffee first then." We approached a server to get a nice strong 4-star hotel Americano, a virtual unknown in India. "Coffee time is over. Hold on." He went to fetch the head server. "Just sit in the lounge it'll just be a moment." Cookies accompanied the coffee.

"Polymath!" The panellists jutted their heads and looked at me.

We were mid-way through the round table discussion making sticky notes and I hadn't said a thing. The word polymath would later find its way into the main presentation. "It's a person who has expertise in more than one area. A renaissance man of sorts. It's hugely important." A sticky note went down into the cluster with polymath on it. I proved myself. I was vetted.

The Heads of Departments and tenured professors continued to make sticky notes as if they were doing round table panel discussions like this every day. But I was included now. My sticky note was in. Months later I would look at a photo of the event, my white skin among a sea of brown. I belonged.

Dispositio

The structure or skeleton of content for my panel discussion invitation was never a consideration. At least, I don't think so. But there I was, waiting... waiting... as ideas came onto the sticky notes and made their way into clusters. A note taker vetted the best ones. Then, as if on the river at a Texas Hold'em table, I went all-in. "Polymath!" I used to be a card player and realized I had internalized that structure. From that point I would limp in, as you do when you are ahead in poker. Did I win? I looked up at the stage seeing the next slide. Design Heads Roundtable discussion. There it was. The word. Polymath.

Wearables

In March 2019, by invitation, I was a speaker in a panel discussion at Vancouver tech company ACL, on "UX [user experience] Design in Wearable Technology."

Greeted by security, up the elevator I went and arrived in an empty space. I looked around for signs of life. None. But this is what I wanted — to feel the space and my presence in it. To know the space, before anyone arrived — before the activity and conversations and Q&A, before the mics and slide decks and banner stands and volunteers — just me and the space. I rummaged through my backpack for my Nike Rogue Ones, the same ones Tim Cook wore when he opened the Apple store in Palo Alto. Eventually organizers started to appear. I put on my Rogues. Luck was on my side now. I sat in the corner as the gears of the event started churning. It had been a while since I'd had such an inviting welcome in Vancouver, and I felt some imposter syndrome as I waited for the other panellists to arrive. "Will there be a photographer?" I asked one of the pink shirts. People started to trickle in, checking in at the makeshift check-in desk. It was a free event and the room would come to fill itself. I hadn't asked about RSVPs. "We're so glad to have you here, Thomas. You're at Emily Carr now, right?" All I could think about was wearables. And how I was going to talk about wearables. I don't remember being particularly nervous, but the nerves always kicked in at events like these. That would never change. I felt like it was my first day of art school again.

"No, no, no, no, no," I blurted out. A knee-jerk reaction. "UX [user experience] should focus on people — why are we emphasizing the technologies?" Blank stare from the moderator. Blank stare from the audience. What was I doing here? Another emotional outburst from Thomas. They continued the panel as if I hadn't said anything. Umph. The discussion floated by and I stared off into the distance. "Are you okay? I'm so sorry!" The moderator approached me afterwards. She was an elementary school teacher by day, completely oblivious to the fact that she was somewhat out of place. "Yeah I'm fine, thank you so much for running this! We were so lucky to have you!"

Elocutio

If we denote vocal modulation with a good talk, I was on the ball. "How can you not think about the people?" I wasn't sure if I was screaming at the audience or the other panellists, or the MC. But I was screaming, screaming at someone. I had been mute the entire time and finally kind of erupted. I was glad to be on the panel but I was also aware that I might have been the only person who was qualified to be there, at least in my mind. I went back to being mute. The MC queued me to respond to a question, I looked around the room. There was Eva, a past student. From then on I would talk as if I was talking to her.

Climate Change

Panel Discussion on "Climate Action" at Emily Carr University of Art + Design, as part of Boma, a global for-profit speaker series where I would emcee.

"I'm thinking of doing something involving a panel discussion down the line..." During preparations for TEDx, Scott, the organizer, was seeding our conversations. I would later come to know that he was hiding a great deal of information from me, information he would use to weave a beautiful story about his second event that he wanted me to be part of. As he finally explained that second event, I admit that I was seduced. But I wanted to do it. I wanted to see Scott succeed. And I wanted the

57

people around me to succeed. And I would do this by raising the bar, by doing this myself. I didn't mind the extra work. But it was only a couple of weeks before the event and everything was still very ambiguous. I sent a disgruntled email asking Scott if he wanted me to emcee this whole thing, explaining that would be a very different beast. "Yes," he said.

Cartem's donuts had already arrived. The beautifully decorated nourishment separating the massive hall from the hallway. The blinds were closed, and Stephanie was there already. She greeted me and I put on my presentation sneakers, preparing for the photography and videography of the event. "We gather on the unceded Coast Salish territory...." I was on autopilot. I wasn't comprehending what I was saying, the words just flowed from inside my corporeal self and out my lips. I was nervous and there were blips and blobs getting in the way of it being a clean introduction.

I quickly turned it over to the select panellists. They were all eager to promote themselves, telling long-winded stories about what they had been experiencing, not so much about climate action but more business in general. They laid it on thick and the audience sat quiet. The room acquired the ambience of a traditional lecture. This wasn't what Scott wanted but this is how it was unfolded. This was supposed to be an experiment. I looked at him and could see his frustration. He was supposed to give me signals. Five minutes. Two minutes. Cut-off. Wrap-up. I interfered as a conductor might guide an orchestra. I was fumbling a bit but they looked to me to move things along, and so I did. I was emceeing.

Memoria

They say that you can't recall it if you never knew it. Sitting down with Scott Mallory at Cartem's Donuts on Main, I sighed a big relief as he pulled up a deck and walked me through what Boma was. It was all new information. "I was thinking you would stand here, and after the first panel you might argue into the student presentations. You might say something like...." I was walking through Olympic Village saying out loud the words Scott spoke to me, internalizing them. There was some improvisation, but basically I was going to say exactly what I remembered Scott saying to me. At times I would deviate, but I would always return to that memory. The coffee shop. And Scott. That was all I knew and all I could draw from. Until the bing of the email client brought me more ideas from Scott. More to draw from. But I was always nervous. Nervous that a next email would come from Scott which would change my ending. Because I couldn't un-remember his advice, which was less advice and more direction to be implemented.

Community Centre

Giving back to 9-14 year olds at Hillcrest Community Centre, Vancouver. "Here's your class list." I wasn't paying attention, my eyes were gliding around the beautiful facade wondering how I ended up here. I was in a daze. I reminded myself that I wasn't getting paid for this. But it didn't matter to me. I was seduced by the architecture of the community centre. I grabbed the list and we walked down the narrow hall, which felt expansive as it overlooked the ice rink, high netting protecting the glass we stood behind from flying pucks.

Eventually we arrived at the room. A worker started pulling out a table. "Let's do a couple of tables and 6 or 7, no let's do 8 chairs," I said. As the chairs were laid out I repositioned them and took out my iPhone to photo document it. I glanced again at the class list, then repositioned the frame of the camera, but again became seduced by the architecture and started cropping in ventilation ducting and exposed beams that lined the ceiling into the photograph. The floor to ceiling windows overlooking the park made their way in as well. I reminded myself that this was a photo of the tables and chairs, and the stack of pink paper, the environment for my workshop.

A small girl dressed all in black sat at a table by herself. Her mom explained to me her trouble communicating in English. "Many people are visual learners," I explained before going into my abstract about the workshop. I talked about the use of time, and how when we are bound by time, interesting things happen. I talked about how we need constraints to be creative, and referred back to the idea that all we use is a piece of paper to make something, without any additional tools. No pen, pencil, tape, glue, nothing. Just your hands and that piece of paper. I also talked about how we were to use some of that hour to make a story about what we made. It could be about design or interaction design, and what you might imagine it to be at this point. They looked up at me. "Can we at least get some pens and pencils or something?"

Actio

It was a snowy day in Vancouver, and I had only one participant. We called them snow days, when everything in Vancouver shut down. It must have been half way through our session when I

60

asked her how old she was. Ten. How do you talk to a ten year old? I rifled through my vocabulary trying to pick accessible, fun, adventurous words. We would go on an adventure together, a journey without leaving that community centre room, without venturing into the snow. My words would take us there. As I picked the words I decided on the journey. I looked at her smiling and realized she could see the destination.

"What's this?" I led. "It's a fish," she said. She spoke in broken English, but I could tell it was an act. She could have made anything she wanted. But it wasn't just a fish, it was a fish of performance, clad with intricate scales, fins that breathed life into the paper. How did my words get us there?

References

- [1] Plato. Gorgias. London: Oxford University Press, 1994.
- [2] Rapp, Christof, "Aristotle's Rhetoric", The Stanford Encyclopedia of Philosophy (Spring 2010 Edition), Edward N. Zalta (ed.), URL = <https://plato.stanford.edu/archives/spr2010/entries/ aristotle-rhetoric/>

GRATITUDE 4: TEDX TRANSCRIPTIONS

English

For as long as I can remember, I've wanted to travel all around the world. But it turns out my favorite places to be are the airports. I realized this was true when I found myself boarding a plane to Seattle just to visit their airport. (Laughter) We often think of the world as a vast place with many unknowns and things to learn about culture, but sometimes we forget the things that can be the same wherever they are in the world. Let me illustrate. Recently, I was on a plane to India, and I was dreaming about India things. Greyish orange skies. The subtropical climate. Haggling over rupees with an auto rickshaw driver in Mumbai. But something happened when I arrived in India. I didn't haggle over rupees. I took a taxi. Another time, I was on my way to Barcelona, and I was dreaming about Barcelona things. Immersed in Gaudi architecture. Eating pan con tomate. Sipping a tempranillo. Something happened there too. I didn't sip a tempranillo. I ordered a Diet Coke. (Laughter)

And a second Diet Coke to save for later. Something happens when we're in unfamiliar situations like these. We seek things that are familiar. We actually crave things that are familiar. Next time you're on a plane, think about some of these things. Think about the Diet Coke. The tomato juice. Christmas. Two-ply toilet paper. Seat belts. Even think about Hollywood movies. And think about how these things might remind you of home. Maybe you'll find yourself on a plane too. Just to visit an airport. Thank you. (Applause)

Spanish

Desde que tengo memoria, he querido viajar alrededor del mundo. Sin embargo, resulta que mis lugares favoritos son los aeropuertos. Me di cuenta de esto cuando me vi abordando un avión a Seattle solo para visitar su aeropuerto. (Risas) Siempre pensamos que el mundo es un enorme lugar con muchas incognitas y cosas culturales que aprender, pero a veces olvidamos las cosas que pueden ser iguales en cualquier parte del mundo. Déjenme mostrarles. Hace poco, estaba en un avión a la India y estaba soñando sobre cosas de la India. Cielos de color naranja grisáceo. El clima subtropical. Regateando rupias con un conductor de autorickshaw en Mumbai. Sin embargo, algo pasó cuando llegué a la India. No regateé rupias. Tomé un taxi. En otra ocasión, estaba volando a Barcelona y soñaba sobre cosas de Barcelona. Inmerso en la arquitectura de Gaudí. Comiendo pan con tomate. Bebiendo un tempranillo. Algo pasó allí también. No bebí un tempranillo. Pedí una Coca Light. (Risas) Y una segunda Coca Light para más tarde. Algo pasa cuando estamos en situaciones desconocidas como estas. Buscamos cosas que son familiares. De hecho anhelamos cosas que son familiares.

La próxima vez que estés en un avión, piensen en alguna de estas cosas. Piensen en la Coca Light. En el jugo de tomate. Navidad. Papel higiénico de dos capas. Cinturones de seguridad. Incluso piensen en las películas de Hollywood. Y piensen en cómo estas cosas podrían recordarles su propio hogar. Quizás también se vean en un vuelo, simplemente para visitar un aeropuerto. Gracias. (Aplausos)

French

D'aussi loin que je me souvienne, j'ai toujours voulu voyager partout dans le monde. Mais en fait, mes endroits préférés sont les aéroports. J'en ai pris conscience lorsque je me suis retrouvé à prendre l'avion pour Seattle, juste pour visiter l'aéroport. (rires) Pour nous, le monde est un vaste endroit rempli d'inconnus et de choses à apprendre sur la culture. Mais parfois, on oublie ces choses qui peuvent être les mêmes où qu'elles soient dans le monde. Je m'explique. Récemment, j'ai pris l'avion pour l'Inde, et je rêvais en pensant à toutes ces images que l'on associe à l'Inde. Le ciel orange tirant sur le gris. Le climat subtropical. Négocier avec le conducteur de pousse-pousse à Mumbai. Mais une fois arrivé en Inde, il s'est passé quelque chose. Je n'ai pas négocié. J'ai pris un taxi. Une autre fois, je me rendais à Barcelone, et je rêvais en pensant à toutes ces images que l'on associe à Barcelone. Me plonger dans l'architecture de Gaudí. Manger du pan con tomate. Siroter un tempranillo. Il s'est passé quelque chose aussi là-bas. Je n'ai pas siroté de tempranillo. J'ai commandé un Coca-Cola Light. (rires) Et un deuxième pour plus tard. Il se passe quelque chose quand on fait face à des situations peu familières. Nous cherchons des choses familières. En fait, on meurt d'envie de retrouver des choses

64

familières. Quand vous prendrez l'avion, pensez à ces choses. Pensez au Coca-Cola Light. Au jus de tomate. A Noël. Au papier toilette double épaisseur. Aux ceintures de sécurité. Pensez même aux films hollywoodiens. Et voyez comment ces choses peuvent vous être familières. Vous vous retrouverez peut-être aussi dans un avion, simplement pour visiter un aéroport. Merci. (applaudissements)

Italian

Fin da quando ho memoria ho sempre voluto viaggiare per il mondo. Ma ho scoperto che i miei posti preferiti sono gli aeroporti. L'ho realizzato quando mi sono ritrovato su di un volo per Seattle solamente per visitare l'aeroporto. (Risate) Pensiamo spesso al mondo come un luogo vasto con molte incognite e nuove cose da imparare riguardo la cultura, ma a volte dimentichiamo le cose che possono essere le stesse in qualunque parte del mondo. Lasciatemi spiegare. Recentemente ero su un aereo per l'India e stavo sognando delle cose indiane. Cieli di un arancio grigiastro, clima subtropicale, contrattare per delle rupie con un pilota di risciò a motore a Mumbai. Ma è successo qualcosa quando sono arrivato in India. Non ho contrattato per le rupie, ho preso un taxi. Un'altra volta, ero in viaggio per Barcellona e stavo sognando le cose di Barcellona. Immersa nell'architettura di Gaudì, mangiando pan con tomate, sorseggiando Tempranillo. Ma è successo qualcosa anche lì. Non ho bevuto Tempranillo, ho ordinato una Diet Coke. (Risate) E un'altra Diet Coke per dopo. Succede qualcosa quando ci si trova in situazioni così insolite. Si cerca ciò che è familiare, veramente si brama ciò che è familiare. La prossima volta che siete su un aereo, pensate ad alcune di queste cose. Pensate

65

alla Diet Coke, la salsa di pomodoro, il Natale, la carta igienica doppio strato, cinture di sicurezza, pensate persino ai film di Hollywood. Pensate a come queste cose potrebbero ricordarvi casa. Magari vi troverete anche voi su un aereo, solamente per visitare un aeroporto. Grazie. (Applausi)

Norwegian

Så lenge jeg kan huske, har jeg ønsket å reise verden rundt. Men det viser seg at favorittstedene mine er flyplassene. Jeg skjønte at dette var sant da jeg fant meg selv ombord på et fly til Seattle bare for å besøke flyplassen deres. (Latter) Vi tenker ofte på verden som et stort sted med mange ukjente og ting å lære om kultur, men noen ganger glemmer vi tingene som kan være de samme uansett hvor de er i verden. La meg illustrere. Nylig var jeg på et fly til India, og jeg drømte om India-ting. Gråaktig oransje himmel. Det subtropiske klimaet. Prute over rupier med en rickshaw-sjåfør i Mumbai. Men noe skjedde da jeg ankom India. Jeg prutet ikke over rupier. Jeg tok taxi. En annen gang, var jeg på vei til Barcelona, og jeg drømte om ting fra Barcelona. Fordypet i Gaudi-arkitektur. Spise pan con tomate. Nipper til en tempranillo. Noe skjedde der også. Jeg nippet ikke til en tempranillo. Jeg bestilte en Diet Coke. (Latter) Og en annen Diet Coke for senere. Noe skjer når vi er i ukjente situasjoner som disse. Vi søker ting som er kjent. Vi lengter faktisk etter ting som er kjent. Neste gang du er på et fly, tenk på noen av disse tingene. Tenk på Diet Coke. Tomatsaften. Jul. To-lags toalettpapir. Setebelter. Tenk på Hollywood-filmer. Og tenk på hvordan disse tingene kan minne deg om hjem. Kanskje du finner deg selv i et fly. Bare for å besøke en flyplass. Takk skal du ha. (Applaus)

Portuguese Brazilian

Desde que me lembro, eu queria viajar ao redor do mundo. Mas acontece que meus lugares favoritos são os aeroportos. Percebi que isso era verdade quando me encontrei embarcando num avião pra Seattle, apenas para visitar o aeroporto de lá. (Risos) Muitas vezes pensamos no mundo como um vasto lugar a ser explorado e cheio de coisas a se aprender sobre cultura, mas às vezes nos esquecemos das coisas que podem ser o mesmo onde quer que estejam no mundo. Deixe-me ilustrar. Recentemente, eu estava em um avião para a Índia, e eu estava sonhando sobre as coisas da Índia. Céus laranja acinzentados. O clima subtropical. Pechinchar rúpias com um motorista de auto-riquixá em Mumbai. Mas algo aconteceu quando cheguei à Índia. Eu não pechinchei rúpias. Eu peguei um táxi. Numa outra vez, eu estava a caminho de Barcelona, e eu estava sonhando com as coisas de Barcelona. Imergir na arquitetura de Gaudi. Comer pão com tomate. Beber um tempranillo. Algo aconteceu lá também. Não bebi um tempranillo. Pedi uma Coca diet. (Risos) E uma segunda Coca diet para mais tarde. Algo acontece quando estamos em situações desconhecidas como estas. Procuramos coisas que são familiares. Realmente ansiamos por coisas que são familiares. Da próxima vez que estiver num avião, pense em algumas dessas coisas. Pense na Coca diet. No suco de tomate. Natal. Papel higiênico de folha dupla. Cintos de segurança. Pense até em filmes de Hollywood. E pense em como essas coisas podem te lembrar de casa. Talvez você se encontre em um avião também. Apenas para visitar um aeroporto. Obrigado. (Aplausos)

Portuguese

Desde que me lembro que queria viajar à volta do mundo. Mas acontece que os meus locais preferido são os aeroportos. Percebi que isto era assim quando me encontrei num avião para Seattle apenas para visitar o aeroporto. (Risos) Muitas vezes pensamos no mundo como um vasto local de coisas desconhecidas e coisas a aprender sobre culturas, mas, por vezes, esquecemos que as coisas podem ser as mesmas onde quer que se encontrem no mundo, Vou ilustrar o que digo. Há pouco tempo, eu ia num avião para a Índia e estava a sonhar com as coisas da Índia. Céus laranja acinzentados, um clima subtropical. Regatear rupias com um condutor de riquexó em Mumbai. Mas aconteceu uma coisa quando cheguei à Índia. Não regateei rupias. Apanhei um táxi. De outra vez, estava a caminho de Barcelona, e sonhava com as coisas em Barcelona. Mergulhado na arquitetura de Gaudi. A comer pão com tomate. A beberricar um "tempranillo". Também ali aconteceu uma coisa. Não beberriquei um "tempranillo". Pedi uma Diet Coke. (Risos) E uma segunda Diet Coke, para daí a bocado. Acontece qualquer coisa quando estamos em situações desconhecidas como estas. Procuramos coisas que conhecemos. Desejamos coisas que são conhecidas. Da próxima vez que estiverem num avião, pensem nalgumas destas coisas. Pensem na Diet Coke. No sumo de tomate. No Natal. No papel higiénico de duas folhas. Nos cintos de segurança. Pensem até nos filmes de Hollywood. Pensem em como essas coisas nos fazem lembrar a nossa terra. Talvez também se encontrem num avião apenas para visitar um aeroporto. Obrigado. (Aplausos)

Swedish

Så länge jag kan minnas, jag har velat resa runt om i världen.

Men det visar sig att mina favoritplatser är flygplatserna. Jag
insåg att detta var sant när jag gick ombord på ett flygplan till
Seattle bara för att besöka deras flygplats. (Skratt) Vi tänker
ofta på världen som en stor plats med många okända faktorer
och saker att lära sig om kultur, men ibland glömmer vi sakerna
det kan vara detsamma var de än är i världen. Låt mig illustrera.
Nyligen var jag på ett plan till Indien och jag drömde om indiska
saker. Grå-orangea himlar. Det subtropiska klimatet. Pruta
över rupier med en motor-rickshawförare i Mumbai. Men något
hände när jag kom till Indien. Jag prutade inte över rupier. Jag
tog en taxi. En annan gång var jag på väg till Barcelona och jag
drömde om Barcelonasaker. Nedsänkt i Gaudi-arkitektur. Äta
spanskt tomatbröd. Smuttar på en tempranillo. Något hände
också där. Jag smuttade inte på någon tempranillo. Jag beställde
en Diet Coke. (Skratt) Och en andra Diet Coke för att spara till
senare. Något händer när vi är i okända situationer som dessa.
Vi söker saker som är bekanta. Vi önskar faktiskt saker som är
bekanta. Nästa gång du är på ett plan tänk på några av dessa
saker. Tänk på Diet Coke. Tomatsaft. Jul. Dubbelt toalettpapper.
Säkerhetsbälten. Tänk även på Hollywood-filmer. Och tänk
på hur dessa saker kanske påminner dig om hemmet. Kanske
märker du också att du sitter på ett plan. Bara för att besöka en
flygplats. Tack. (Applåder)

Turkish

Kendimi bildim bileli dünyayı dolaşmak istiyorum. Anlaşıldı ki
en sevdiğim yerler havaalanları. Kendimi yalnızca havaalanını
görmek için Seattle'a uçak bileti ararken bulduğumda bunu
fark ettim. (Kahkaha) Genelde dünyayı birçok bilinmeyeni ve
öğrenilecek kültürel birçok şeyi olan bir yer olarak düşünüyoruz.

69

ancak bazen dünyanın her yerinde aynı olan şeyleri unutuyoruz. Açıklayayım. Geçtiğimiz günlerde Hindistan'a giden bir uçaktaydım ve Hindistan'a özgü şeyleri düşünüyordum. Griye çalan turuncu gökyüzü. Subtropikal iklim. Mumbai'de bir üç tekerlekli sürücüsüyle pazarlığa tutuşmak. Ama Hindistan'a vardığımda bir şeyler oldu. Üç tekerlekliler için pazarlığa tutuşmadım. Bir taksi tuttum. Başka bir zaman da Barselona yolundayken Barselona'ya özgü şeyleri düşünüyordum. Gauidi mimarisine dalıp gitmiştim. Pan con tomate yemek. Tempranillo içmek. Orada da bir şeyler oldu. Tempranillo içemedim. Diyet kola sipariş ettim. (Kahkaha) Daha sonra içmek için bir tane daha söyledim. Böyle alışılmadık durumlarda hep bir şeyler olur zaten. Alıştığımız bir şeylerin peşine düşeriz. Alıştığımız şeyleri çeker canımız. Bir daha ki sefere bir uçağa bindiğinizde bunları bir düşünün. Diyet kolayı bir düşünün. Domates suyunu. Noeli. İki katlı tuvalet kağıdını. Emniyet kemerlerini. Hatta Hollywood filmlerini. Böyle şeylerin size nasıl evi hatırlattığını bir düşünün. Belki bir gün siz de kendinizi bir uçakta bulursunuz, sırf bir havaalanını görmek için bindiğiniz bir uçakta. Teşekkürler. (Alkış)

Greek

Από τότε που θυμάμαι τον εαυτό μου, ήθελα να ταξιδέψω σε όλον τον κόσμο. Αλλά τελικά τα αγαπημένα μου μέρη είναι τα αεροδρόμια. Το συνειδητοποίησα όταν βρέθηκα να επιβιβάζομαι σε ένα αεροπλάνο για το Σιάτλ μόνο και μόνο για να επισκεφτώ το αεροδρόμιό τους. (Γέλια) Συχνά σκεφτόμαστε τον κόσμο ως ένα αχανές μέρος με πολλά άγνωστα και πράγματα που αξίζει να μάθουμε για τους πολιτισμούς, αλλά μερικές φορές ξεχνάμε αυτά που μπορεί να είναι τα ίδια όπου και να βρίσκονται στον κόσμο. Θα σας δώσω ένα παράδειγμα. Πρόσφατα, πέταγα για Ινδία, και ονειρευόμουν πράγματα σχετικά με την Ινδία. Γκριζοπορτοκαλί ουρανούς. Το υποτροπικό κλίμα. Να κάνω παζάρια σε ρουπίες με έναν οδηγό τρίκυκλου στη Μουμπάι. Αλλά κάτι συνέβη όταν έφτασα στην Ινδία. Δεν έκανα παζάρια σε ρουπίες. Πήρα ένα ταξί. Μια άλλη φορά, πήγαινα στη Βαρκελόνη, και ονειρευόμουν πράγματα σχετικά με την Βαρκελόνη. Να βυθίζομαι στην αρχιτεκτονική του Γκαουντί. Να τρώω ψωμί με ντομάτα. Να πίνω κρασί Τεμπρανίγιο. Αλλά κάτι συνέβη κι εκεί. Δεν ήπια Τεμπρανίγιο. Παράγγειλα Coca Cola Light. (Γέλια) Και μια δεύτερη Coca Cola Light για μετά. Κάτι συμβαίνει όταν βρισκόμαστε σε άγνωστες καταστάσεις όπως αυτή. Αναζητούμε αυτά που μας είναι γνώριμα. Στην πραγματικότητα, λαχταρούμε αυτά που μας είναι γνώριμα. Την επόμενη φορά που θα είστε σε ένα αεροπλάνο, σκεφτείτε μερικά από αυτά. Σκεφτείτε την Coca Cola Light. Τον τοματοχυμό. Τα Χριστούγεννα. Το διπλό χαρτί υγείας. Τις ζώνες ασφαλείας. Σκεφτείτε μέχρι και τις Χολιγουντιανές ταινίες. Και σκεφτείτε πώς αυτά τα πράγματα σας θυμίζουν το σπίτι σας. Ίσως να βρεθείτε κι εσείς πάνω σε ένα αεροπλάνο. Απλώς για να επισκεφτείτε ένα αεροδρόμιο. Σας ευχαριστώ. (Χειροκρότημα)

Russian

Сколько я себя помню, я всегда хотел путешествовать по миру. Но оказывается, мои любимые места — аэропорты. Я понял это, когда садился в самолёт в Сиэтле, — просто чтобы побыть в аэропорту. (Смех) Мы часто представляем мир огромным, неизведанным, с культурными различиями, но иногда забываем о вещах, которые похожи, где бы они ни находились. Приведу наглядный пример. Недавно я летел в Индию и мечтал о том, что я там увижу. Серовато-оранжевое небо. Субтропический климат. Спор из-за стоимости поездки с водителем рикши в Мумбае. Но что-то произошло, когда я приехал в Индию. Я не спорил по поводу цены поездки. Я взял такси. В другой раз, по пути в Барселону, я представлял себя в Барселоне погружённым в архитектуру Гауди, жующим хлеб с помидорами и потягивающим темпранильо. Но и там кое-что произошло. Я не пил темпранильо. Я заказал диетическую колу. (Смех) И вторую, такую же, я оставил на потом. Что-то происходит, когда мы в незнакомых ситуациях, подобных этим. Мы ищем привычные нам вещи. На самом деле мы мечтаем о знакомых нам вещах. В следующий раз, находясь на борту самолёта, подумайте о них. Подумайте о диетической коле, о томатном соке, Рождестве, двухслойной туалетной бумаге, о ремнях безопасности и даже о голливудских фильмах. И подумайте, как эти вещи могут напоминать вам о доме. Может, и вы тоже окажетесь в самолёте, только чтобы побывать в аэропорту. Спасибо. (Аплодисменты)

Arabic

ما استطعت عع تذكرك، أني طالما أدردت السفر حول العالم. ولكن
اتحضر أن الألمكن المفضلة لدي هي المطارات. أدركت أن هذا
صحيح عندما وجدت نفسي أصعد طائرة إلى سيايتل فقط

72

لزيارة مطارهم. (ضحك) كثيرا ما نفكر في العالم كمكان واسع
مع المجهودين والأشياء لنتعلمها عن الثقافة، لكن في
بعض الأحيان ننسى الأشياء التي يمكن أن تكون هي نفسها
دعوني أو وأخرا، مؤخرا. حضر. تكونوا في العالم. أينما تكونوا على متن
طائرة إلى الهند، وكنت أحمل بالأشياء الهندية. سماء بترقاقلية
والمخانق شب شبه الاستوائي. والمساومة على الروبية مع
رمادية. والمخانق شب شبه الاستوائي. والمساومة على الروبية مع
سائق عربة الريكشا في مومباي. لكن كنت حدث شيء ما عندما وصلت
إلى الهند. لم أساس على روبية. وأخذت تاكسي. مرة أخرى،
كنت في طريقي إلى بربرشلون، وكنت تكنت أحمل بأشياء بربرشلونة.
أغمس نفسي في معمار المصمم غاودي. آوآى لكل الخبز مع الطماطم.
واحتست نبيذ التمبرنيو. وحدث شيئا ما هناك أيضا. لم
احتست نبيذ التمبرنيو. وطلبت مشروب حميم غازية. (ضحك)
وعلبة مشروب حميم غازية أخرى لوقت لاحق. شيء ما يحدث عندما
نمر بمواقف غير مألوفة مثل هذه. نبحث عن المألوف. نحن في
الواقع نتطلع إلى الأشياء المألوفة. في المرة القادمة عندما
فكروا. كفكروا في بعض هذه الأشياء. تكونوا على متن طائرة، فكروا
في مشروب حميم الغازي. وعصير الطماطم. عيد الميلاد. ورورق
التوالتي ذي الطبقتين. نبتفتين. أحزمة المقاعد. فكروا حتى في
فلام هوليوود. وفكروا في كيفية أن هذه الأشياء قد تذكركم
بمنازلكم. ربما تستجدون أنفسكم على متن طائرة أيضا. فقط
لتزوروا المطار. شكرا لكم. (تصفيق)

Kurdish

ههات بیرم و سیستووهمه گه شت به ههمموو جهیهاندا به که‌م.
ههئ پیرم و سیستووهمه گه شت به ههمموو جهیهاندا به که‌م.
بههڵام ئهوه درکرهوه که شوونهیشقوخ مناکه بۆ چم
زانی ئهمهم راست کاته کئ خۆم دیهوه فرزکخانهکانن.
دانیشتووم له وان فرزکۆکه هیهک بۆ سیاتل تهنها بۆ سهردانی

73

ناھیج ەل ریب راجرۆز ەمئئ (نینەکئپ) .نایەکەناخەکۆزف
وارسانەن نیەدندىن چەگەل ەروە گ ى کئنئىوش کەو ەوەنىەکەدە
کئەدنەە مالّەب ،روتلىک یەراب رەد نووبریئ ۆب ناکەتش و
تئئ بت ش نامەە تئرکەدە ەک نىەکەدە ریبەلەل ناکەتش راج
مەل .ەوەمەکبئنوور نم اب .نن ەناھىج مئئ ى کەیئی کەرە ەل
منوەخ نم و ،ناتسدنيە ۆب مووب کەیەکۆزف ەل ،ادەنایایاود
یلّاقەتەرپ ینامسئائ .ناتسدنيە ىناکەتش یەراب رەد نىیەبەدە
ینانگرزاب .ىیەگلوخ ەچمىئن یاوەە و ەشەک .ىشئەمەلّۆخ
.یابۆّمۆم ەل رئگتەسەد یرئۆفۆش لەگەل یپوور یەراپ ەب
نم .ناتسدنيە ەمتشىەگ کئتّاک ادیوور کئتت شە مالّەب
.تىرگ مکەییسکات نم .درکەن ى پوور ى ەراپ ەب ەب مادوەس
ەب منوەخ و ،ەنۆلّەشرەب ۆب مووب ەگئر ەل نم ،رت ى کئئراج
ییزاسرالەت وان ەموچ .ىننیەبەدە ەوەنۆلّەشرەب ىناکەتش
ئئەوەل .ىبارەش ەل ى کئنمۆق .دراوخ ەمتامەە و نان .ىدۆگ
یاواد نم .ادەن ۆلىنەرپمئئت ەل مموق نم .ادیوور رت ى کئئ تش
یەوەندراوخ ەموود (نینەکئپ) .درکە تیاد ى کۆک یەوەندراوخ
تادەدوور کئئت ش .تىزئرابىب رتاوەد یەوەئ ۆب تىاد ى کۆک ى
یاوەدب ەمئئ .نیەرۆج ەل نا کناوابان ەتەلّاح ەل ەمئئ کئئتاکاش
ىۆزرەە یتسارەبوب ەمئئ .نواب ەک نىئ رەگەدە ادەناتش ەوەئ
ریب ،تىادەکۆزف ەل ەک ووتاەادا یراج .نواب ەک نىناکەتش
ى کۆک یەوەندراوخ ەل ریب .ەوەکب ەناتش مەل کئئدنەە ەل
یەنوور کىادەل یئنۆەج .ەتامەە ىتەبرەە ش .ەوەکب تىاد
تەناناەت .ىەروک ىنئئتەش پ .تىئلّاوەت ىسنئئل ک .ح ىسەم
ەوەنەکب ەوەل ریب .ەوەنەکب شىدووىلّۆزە ىملیف ەل ریب
ەیەناوەل .ەوەنئئەبریب تەوەلّامّ ەیەناوەل ەناتش مئئ نۆچ ەک
یناندەرەس ۆب ەنەت .ەوەتىزۆزدب شى کەیەکۆزف ەل تۆخ
(نادئل ەلّپەچ) .ساپ وس .کەیەناخەکۆزف

Hindi

जहाँ तक मुझे याद है, मुझे पूरा वश्वि भ्रमण करना था। लेकनि जाहिरा तौर पर

मेरे पसंदीदा स्थान हवाई अड्डे हैं। मुझे एहसास हुआ कि यह सच था जब मैं सिएटल के लिए एक विमान में सवार हुआ बस उनके हवाई अड्डे का दौरा करने के लिए। (हँसी) हम अक्सर विश्व के बारे में सोचते हैं कई अज्ञात लोगों के साथ एक विशाल स्थान के रूप में और संस्कृति के बारे में सिखने लेकिन कभी-कभी हम समान चीजों को भूल जाते हैं वे दुनिया में जहा भी हों। मैं एक दृष्टांत के साथ समझाऊंगा। हाल ही में, मैं भारत गया था, और मैं सपना देख रहा था भारत की चीजों के बारे में। ग्रे नारंगी आसमान। उपोष्णकटिबंधीय जलवायु। रुपयों के भाव ताव करते हुए एक ऑटो रिक्शा चालक के साथ मुंबई में। लेकिन कुछ हुआ जब मैं भारत आया। मैंने रुपयों से मोल तोल नहीं किया। मैंने टैक्सी ली। एक और बार, मैं था बार्सिलोना के लिए मेरे रास्ते पर, और मैं बार्सिलोना की चीजों के बारे में सपने देख रहा था। गौड़ी वास्तुकला में डूबा हुआ। पान कोन टमाटर खाते हुए। टेंपरामिलो की चुस्की लेते हुए वहां भी कुछ हुआ। मैंने टेंपरामिलो की चुस्की नहीं ली। मैंने आहार कोक मंगाया। (हँसी) और बाद में एक और आहार कोक। अपरिचित स्थितियों में ऐसा कुछ होता हैं। हम परिचित चीजों की तलाश करते हैं। हम वास्तव में परिचित चीजों को तरसते हैं, अगली बार जब आप विमान में हों, इन कुछ चीजों के बारे में सोचें। डाइट कोक के बारे में सोचें। टमाटर का रस। क्रिसमस। टू-प्लाई टॉयलेट पेपर। सीट बेल्ट। हॉलीवुड फिल्मों के बारे में भी सोचें। और इन चीजों के बारे में सोचें जो आपको घर की याद दिला सकता है। हो सकता है कि आप खुद को एक विमान पर भी पाएं। बस एक हवाई अड्डे पर जाने के लिए। धन्यवाद। (तालियां)

Japanese

ついたからずっとはをしたいとってきましたでもでかったのおにりの
です このにづいたのは シアトルきのにって ただをれたでした
は くのにれ をぶべきものにちただと たちはしがちですが
として れてしまうのは のどこにってもじょうなことがこりる
ということです つまり こういうことです インドへかうで が
ていたのは インドっぽいものでしたの ルピーをに タクシーのに
ムンバイでりです でも インドにしたら あることがこりました
はりをせずのタクシーにったのですまたのに バルセロナにかうで

75

はバルセロナっぽいものを ていました ガウディーのにになり
パ・アム・トゥマカットをベ テンプラニーリョをっていました
ここでも あることがこりました テンプラニーリョをらず
したのはダイエットコーラと でむためののコーラですこのようなれない
ちょっとしたことがこります たちは れたものをめます は
れたものをするのです さんもににるときは してみてさい えば
ダイエット・コーラ トマトジュース クリスマス ねのトイレットペーパー
シートベルト そしてハリウッドも そしてそれらがさんにとって
どれ みがあるかしてさい あなたもにっているかもしれません
ただ にくためだけに ありがとうございました

About the Author

BIO

Thomas Girard (born 30 December, 1980 in Vancouver, Canada) is a Canadian scholar. Girard was accepted to attend University of Oxford in lectures equivalent to graduate coursework. Girard has received several Emerging Scholar awards, first at the Design Principles and Practices conference in Barcelona, Spain at the prestigious ELISAVA. At Emily Carr University of Art and Design he received his second Emerging Scholar award. Other awards include RBC Emerging Scholar, Royal Bank of Canada Foundation. For 2021, he has been awarded an Emerging Scholar award from the New Directions in the Humanities conference in Madrid, Spain.

You can connect with me on:
- http://www.thomaskgirard.com
- http://www.twitter.com/onthomas_tweet

CPSIA information can be obtained
at www.ICGtesting.com
Printed in the USA
BVHW070721130921
616359BV00009B/217